Wizards Are a Nuisance

"The Second Assistant Herald tacked a large notice on the Palace notice board, hit his thumb and said 'Ow!' dropped the hammer on his foot and said 'Ow! Ow!' banged his head on the notice board in picking up the hammer and said 'Ow! Ow! Ow!'"

The notice announced a Grand Contest for the position of Court Wizard to the Kingdom of Hullaboolania.

The contest which followed was fought frantically, fiercely and frightfully until the audience was in a greater uproar than the Wizards from the complications of mixed-up magic which missed and splintery spells which splashed. The Dukes, Duchesses, Lords and Ladies who found themselves with extra long noses, too many ears or striped hair all agreed that Wizards *are* a nuisance!

This Jackanory original has four more Wizard stories by that Master of Magic, Norman Hunter, together with Quentin Blake's delightfully dotty drawings.

WIZARDS ARE A NUISANCE

NORMAN HUNTER

ILLUSTRATED BY QUENTIN BLAKE

British Broadcasting Corporation

Published by the British Broadcasting Corporation,
35 Marylebone High Street, London W1M 4AA
ISBN 0 563 12402 4
First published 1973

Printed in England by John Blackburn Ltd, Leeds

Wizards are a Nuisance

The Second Assistant Royal Herald tacked a large notice on the Palace notice board, hit his thumb and said "Ow!", dropped the hammer on his foot and said "Ow! Ow!" banged his head on the notice board in picking up the hammer and said "Ow! Ow! Ow!"

This is what the notice said:

GRAND CONTEST OF
MAGIC
FOR THE POSITION OF
COURT WIZARD
TO THE KINGDOM OF
HULLABOOLANIA

PERCIVAL PRETTYPOTION
VERSUS
SILAS SCATTERSPELLZ

TO BE HELD IN THE
PALACE GROUNDS
NEXT MONDAY AT 3 PM
PRECISELY

DECK CHAIRS 6P SIT-ON-THE-GROUND 2P

Next Monday the palace grounds were fuller than a football match. Everybody was so excited about the contest that the King's guards had to let off several enormous cannon to get enough silence for the Chief Herald to announce the contest, and to say that there would be twelve rounds and that if either contestant should make himself invisible he would be disqualified.

"I hope they're better than that conjurer we had last Christmas," whispered the Queen. "It took until thirteenth night to clear up the mess of confetti and bran and tissue paper he made on the carpet."

"Urrg," said the King, who had his mouth full of chocolate creams he'd brought, as he found it very difficult to watch anything for long without something to eat.

Then a trumpet sounded for the start of the contest.

Percival Prettypotion, a tall skinny wizard with long waving fingers, was

dressed in a long robe covered in coloured cats and wore a pointed hat with a dent in it where he'd sat on it by mistake.

Silas Scatterspellz was rather round and slightly fat, wore short trousers, long boots, a wide hat and narrow whiskers. He let go a heavy spell at Percy to turn him into a frog, but Percy batted it back and made a shrink-you-small incantation at Silas, which missed and shrunk the King's chocolate creams into weeny dots.

"Foul!" cried the King. "Disqualify him."

"No, no," cried the Chief Herald, "contest continues."

"Have one of my ridiculously strong peppermints," said the Queen, but the King shook his head and hoped perhaps a later spell would make his chocolate creams big again and perhaps more of them.

Then Percy threw a set of magic railings round Silas. Silas made a gate in them but as he walked out Percy turned himself into a soldier with a fixed bayonet and barred his way. Instantly Silas became an officer and ordered Percy to stand back, Percy became a patch of squishy mud that stuck Silas to the ground, Silas became a dragon-fly and flew up out of the mud, above the fence. But boom! Percy was an anti-aircraft gun trying to shoot down Silas. His first shot missed and knocked a turret off the palace.

"Thank goodness for that," said the Queen, "one room less to dust and four windows less to clean."

"Go it Silas!" roared half the crowd,

throwing their hats in the air.

"Paralyse him Percy!" cried the other half, waving ice-cream cones and bags of crisps.

Before Percy could fire again, Silas turned himself into another gun, they both fired down each other's barrels, there was an enormous bang , coloured smoke and tin stars, then both guns vanished and Percy and Silas with scorched eyebrows and Silas with sizzled whiskers, were

bowing to the applause as the trumpet sounded for the end of Round One.

Five Earls and seven Duchesses took off their coronets and started on the sandwiches they'd brought in them. The Queen opened a new packet of peppermints. The King would have sent

for another box of chocolate creams only all the shops were shut as everyone was at the contest.

Tan-tara went the trumpet and Round Two began with Silas slamming a heavy spell at Percy. Pwouff! Where was Percy?

"Made himself invisible?" asked the King.

"No, no, Majesty, dried pea Majesty," said the Chief Herald peering through a magnifying glass as a little green pea Percy went rolling along the ground.

Then Silas turned himself into a bird to

eat up the pea. But he stamped his foot. "Bother!" he chirped. He'd made himself into a bird that didn't like peas.

Then Percy changed into a cat and pounced on the bird. Silas became a dog, Percy became a bigger dog. Snarls broke out. Silas became a bucket of burning coal, then Percy turned into a bucket of water and poured himself into Silas. There was a loud hiss, a cloud of steam and Percy and Silas emerged soaking wet and looking rather silly as the trumpet went for the end of that round.

By this time plenty of the audience had extra long noses, or too many ears, or striped hair, where stray spells had hit them. Several deck chairs had collapsed and there was some argument as to whether a collapsed deck chair counted as a 6p deck chair or a 2p sit-on-the-ground.

"It's all very clever I'm sure," said the Queen opening another new packet of even fiercer peppermints, "but I don't see how it helps with the housework."

Tan-tara went the trumpet and instantly Percy Prettypotion multiplied himself into fifteen Percys and surrounded Silas. Silas shot out a spell and shrunk all the Percys into little ones two inches high.

"Ra ra ra ra!" yelled the crowd.

Silas started stamping on the little Percys, one, two, three, four, five.

Ten more deck chairs collapsed. Marchionesses and Viscounts and Dukes clambered onto one another's shoulders to see better.

"Sit down," shouted the crowd.

Stamp stamp thump bonk! Four more little Percys done for.

The Chief Herald was dancing round like a crazy grasshopper, trying to keep count of things.

At last only one little two-inch Percy was left. Silas swelled himself up to ten-feet high and lifted his huge foot.

"Silas wins," yelled the Silas half of the crowd.

But, *whoosh*! Percy managed to get out a a spell at the last split second and changed himself into a very spiky rock. Silas couldn't stop himself and brought his foot down bang on the rock.

"Ow! Ow! OW!" he yelled much louder than the Assistant Herald had yelled when he hit his thumb, because he was much bigger.

Then Percy became a big bird and started pecking Silas. Silas changed to a cat and the trumpet went just in time to stop them going all through the dog, bigger dog, bucket of fire, bucket of water routine they'd done before.

"I do hope you see that they put right all the damage they've done," said the

Queen, looking at her packet of peppermints, that had changed into a jar of unsuccessful home-made marmalade.

Tan-tara went the trumpet again.

Then something highly complicated happened. Silas Scatterspellz changed himself into Percival Prettypotion and at the same time Percy turned himself into Silas.

"Oh dear, now we shall never know who's won," groaned the Queen.

Then Silas, or was it Percy, turned the contest ground into a pond and made a huge tidal wave bear down on Percy, or rather Silas.

Then Silas or Percy or whichever it was, magicked up a motor boat and came at Percy/Silas, who sank it with an enchanted torpedo and Percy or Silas turned into a fish. Then came the end of the round and for a moment there were two Percys sitting in one corner until Silas remembered who he was and changed back to himself. By now there was uproar in the audience as nobody knew whose side he was on.

"Stop the contest," cried the King "and ask these two gentlemen to get the audience calmed down and sorted out."

So Silas and Percy, both on the same side for the moment, released a few carefully-chosen magics and settled the squabbling audience into neat rows again with very chewy and stick-your-teeth-together kind of toffee and ice-creams all round, to keep them quiet.

"The contest may continue," said the Queen, graciously waving a hand and upsetting the marmalade over the King. But the King just said "Urgg," because he'd started on the chewy toffee the wizards had landed on his hand, without thinking, and couldn't say anything else.

Then the contest began again. But it hadn't gone more than two spells and half an incantation when Silas did the most outrageous thing. Yes, yes, he made Percy invisible. Oh disgraceful thing! Oh dreadful situation!

Because the rules said if either of them made himself invisible he would be disqualified and the other one would win. Silas made Percy invisible, but the Herald and the King and Queen and all the audience thought it was Percy who had disappeared himself. So poor invisible innocent Percy was disqualified and Silas was declared the winner.

"Well I must say that was most interesting," said the Queen, "better than the pictures and nothing to pay."

"Urgg," said the King still fastened down around the teeth by the toffee.

For two outrageous days Silas Scatterspellz had been Court Magician. The King, after Silas had magicked his teeth free of the toffee, had given him handsome robes, purple ones with yellow fringes and fancy stars. He had a magic wand with flashing lights and a hat that changed colour ten times a day except on Sundays.

Of course he had no right to these things. He had cheated poor old Percy. Disgraceful! Was there no justice?

Well there were certainly a lot of other things. For Percy Prettypotion was making himself no end of an invisible nuisance. He couldn't make himself visible again because Silas's spell was too strong, but he kept moving the furniture into silly places. He made the Queen spill her tea. "There, look what you've made me do," she'd say to the King, who was at the other end of the royal table and didn't see how he could have, but knew it was no use arguing.

So he sent for Silas.

"Look here," said his Majesty, wagging a royal finger at Silas, "this won't do you know. You win the contest and we are graciously pleased to appoint you Court Magician, but we are most *un*graciously displeased at the things you are doing. Yesterday the grand piano was in the bathroom. The day before, my bed was filled with marbles. Then this morning the sugar basin turned into a mouse and ran up the curtains. Very entertaining no doubt for people who like that kind of thing, but highly unsuitable for a royal

palace. What do you mean by it, eh, tell me that?"

"I-er-um-ah," mumbled Silas. He knew jolly well it was invisible Percy who was doing all these undesirable things, but of course he couldn't say so. He was Court Magician. He was supposed to be able to see that unrequired magic did not occur.

"I will see to it Majesty," he said, "something shall be done about it."

"It better had, or had better, or whatever is the right way to say it," grunted the King, and he stalked off straight through a puddle Percy had put down to catch Silas.

"Pah!" snorted the King. "You're dismissed do you hear? You are no longer Court Magician."

"Does that mean I can be Court Magician?" gabbled Percy, from behind the umbrella stand. "I was cheated, I didn't make myself invisible, he did it." He pointed a long skinny finger at Silas, but of course the King couldn't see it.

"What do you think you're talking about?" demanded the King, who couldn't see invisible Percy and thought it was Silas talking. "And don't put on that silly voice to me."

"I-er-er-er," mumbled Silas thinking forty miles an hour but not being able to think of what to do about things.

"I know you err," said the King, "and I'm tired of your erring all over the place. It's most inconvenient. Stop it at once.

You're dismissed. Leave the Palace immediately and take your magic with you."

"But Majesty," cried Silas, and he was so scared of being dismissed and so muddled up trying to think what to do, he let his spell on Percy slip a bit.

Instantly Percy shot up all visible in front of the King.

"What are you doing here!" thundered the King. "You cheated. You were disqualified. How dare you come here!"

"He-he-he-he-he," stuttered Percy, pointing at Silas, "he-he-he-"

"Don't you laugh at me," roared the King, who thought all that he he-ing was Percy laughing.

"I'm not laughing," cried Percy. "I did not cheat, it is I who was cheated."

"You made yourself invisible against the rules," cried the King.

"No, no, *no*, Majesty," protested Percy. "He made me invisible."

"What's that?" said the King, not believing his ears, though he'd never known them tell lies before.

"He made me invisible to win the contest," said Percy. "I have been doing all the magic to draw attention to myself."

"Ho," said the King, "so pianos in bathrooms and expensive marbles in King's beds are your doing are they? Off with your head."

"Yes, Majesty, I agree Majesty," gabbled Silas rubbing his hands. "I'll fetch the Executioner."

"I shall only put it back again you know," said Percy. "Offing with a Wizard's head is a waste of time."

"Pah!" snorted the King again. "You're both dismissed. Go away. Leave at once, and never come here again."

Percy and Silas began a hurried secret sort of whispering. Then Silas said: "Pardon Majesty, we have a plan."

"There is a way out of the difficulty that will satisfy us all," added Percy.

"I know there is," shouted the King, "you both get out, you and your magic."

"Er, no Majesty," said Silas, "we have

a better idea. Let us *share* the post of Court Magician. We will agree not to do any magic without your Majesty's approval. And your Majesty will have the distinction of being the only King to have not one Court Magician but two. The other kingdoms will be bright green with envy."

"Er-ah-um," said the King, thinking a bit.

"And with two of us on your side," put in Percy, "no magician from a rival kingdom will have a chance of doing any mischief."

"Well-er," said the King, considering like mad.

Just then the Queen came sweeping in. "Henry," she said in her special do-as-I-tell-you voice, "I positively must have a new dress for the royal banquet next week, whether we can afford it or not."

"But my dear," said the King.

"What colour would your Majesty like?" asked Silas bowing low.

"Silk or velvet?" enquired Percy, bowing lower.

"What's that?" said the Queen. It was her turn not to believe her ears now.

Then the King saw daylight, quantities of it, complete with bright sunshine and all the trimmings.

"Why of course, my dear, certainly my dear," he said, smiling right across his face, "of course you must have a new dress for the banquet! And a new diamond tiara and earrings, to say nothing of pearls and rubies to wear."

He looked enquiringly at Silas and Percy, who both bowed so low they nearly split their breeches.

"Diamond tiara by all means Majesty," they said. "Earrings of course. Pearls and rubies naturally and emeralds as well if Her Majesty is so inclined."

The Queen opened her mouth without saying anything, a thing she hadn't done for years.

"Carry on Wizards," said the King regally, "and while you're at it, I need a new smoking jacket. Crimson velvet trimmed with gold braid and sapphire buttons."

"Certainly Majesty," chorused the two Wizards.

So the wizard situation was saved. And the Queen spent the rest of the day thinking up rows and rows of extraordinary hats for Percy and Silas to magic up for her.

The Ice-Cream-Van Wizard

Ting a ling, ting a ling, clang clang dong. Down the main street of Upper Downton came an ice-cream sort of van. It was bright mauve with pink ornaments. It was drawn by a tame striped dragon. And it played the most astonishing music as it went along.

Only it wasn't an ice-cream van at all. It had printed on the sides in very loud letters:

"Ha ha," cried William J Waveywand, the Wizard who was driving the van, "this was a jolly good idea of mine was this, this was and all."

Suddenly out of a side street shot an excited somebody waving his hands about while the wind waved his hair about.

"Stop stop!" he cried. "I want to buy a magic."

It was the Duke of Diddinot Dooso.

"Whoa!" cried the wizard pulling on the reins, and the dragon drew up with loud puffings and clouds of coloured steam.

"Ha ha ha," panted the Duke, "have you some kind of spell or magic of some kind that will make fat people slim?" he asked. "The Duchess, you see," he explained, "is rather, er – well that is to say she is a little on the er-er-"

"She's fat?" asked the wizard who never minced his words, perhaps because he hadn't got a word mincer.

"Yes, yes," said the Duke. "She is most decidedly fat, only it doesn't seem very polite to say so. She's tried everything she can think of to make herself slim, except putting herself through the mangle. She didn't try that because we haven't a mangle, only a spin drier, which I don't

think would have had the right effect."

"No, no, indeed no," said William J Waveywand, who thought the idea of a spin-dried Duchess was too unreasonable to think about. "But I have the very thing here."

He rummaged about among his spells and magics. He scattered packages and tins and bottles all over the place. At last he found what he was looking for, after looking for it wherever it wasn't. He handed the Duke a pink packet that

looked like a shampoo powder and smelt like old rubber boots burning slowly.

"Shake this powder over the Duchess," he said, "then read out the spell you will find printed on the wrapping paper. Soon Her Grace will be nice and slim."

"I hope it works," said the Duke. He paid for the packet and went running back, while William J Waveywand started up his dragon and drove his musical magic wagon away down the street.

Presently he came to a nice quiet part, stopped his wagon, gave the dragon a bowl of flaming peanuts to eat and started checking his stock of spells and incantations.

"Spells to make fat people slim," he said, looking in his little black book, where he kept a list of his magic, "I had six when I started out today, I sold one to the Duke so I should have five left." He counted the packets:

"One, two, three, four, five, six." He let out a shriek that nearly put the dragon off his peanuts. "Goblins and breadcrumbs!" he cried. "I must have sold the wrong spell to the Duke."

Feverishly he counted over the other spells. He sorted out sorceries. He investigated incantations. He checked the conjurations.

"Worse than I feared, which I didn't think was possible," he wailed. "Oh, what a careless wizard I am! I've sold a spell to make tall people short. Oh dreadful disaster! Oh miserable muddle-up!"

It was certainly all that and probably more. Instead of the too fat Duchess going all nice and slim, the magic spell would make her even fatter. She would be broader than she was long – which is awful for anyone, let alone a Duchess. People would start calling her Your Great instead of Your Grace.

"I must stop the Duke before he gives her the magic," cried William J. He pushed his spells back into the van, and snatched the peanut bowl away from the dragon. He leapt into the driver's seat.

"Off, away, hurry, speed, hot foot, whatsname for leather, faster faster!" he yelled. Then he suddenly gave a gasp and shouted: "Whoa, stop, come back, as you were."

The dragon blew out five sorts of coloured steam, snorted like ten fire engines that smelt a blaze, dug his claws into the road and nearly choked on his last peanut, trying to do all these things at once.

"Careful careful," gasped William J

Waveywand, "never do to arrive at Duke's palace like this. Too noticeable. People will talk. Must get there all secretly." He talked like a money-saving telegram because he didn't feel there was time to talk ordinarily.

He climbed down from the van. Patted the dragon. Wished he hadn't because he burnt his fingers. Said a spell that turned dragon and van into a nice quiet not-at-all-noticeable scooter driven by nice quiet elastic and went whizzing off for the Duke's castle.

Up the hill he dashed, urging the scooter on with magic incantations that made no difference. Three times he had a puncture – but mended it magically. Twice he sideslipped into the gutter – but thank goodness it was dry. *Whiz-whiz slipetty-blip* the scooter carried him up to the castle. Wow! The drawbridge was down, thank goodness. He shot across it, through the main gate, leapt off the scooter but forgot to stop it. Ran like mad after it, then remembered just in time and stopped it with a stopping spell, when it fell into a bed of geraniums.

"Oh dear, this is awful," he gasped. "Why ever did I become a wizard? Why wasn't I an engine driver or a space-man or something quiet and unexciting like that?"

He tore into the castle, rushed from room to room, clambered up endless winding staircases. Galloped through galleries.

"The Duke!" he cried. "Where is the Duke?"

Alas, he couldn't find the Duke, but suddenly he found the Duchess. She was asleep on an enormous couch with an elegant cup of tea beside her.

"Oh dear, oh dear," cried the wizard, "the making-short magic has begun to work."

As a matter of fact it had done nothing of the kind. The wizard had shot back to the castle so quickly he'd got there before the Duke, who'd stopped for a glass of lemonade and several chocolate biscuits on the way. But William J Waveywand didn't know that. How could he? The Duke had told him the Duchess was fat, which she certainly was. But he hadn't told him she was short, which she also certainly was. And William J, seeing such a short stumpy Duchess on the couch, instantly guessed the worst and guessed absolutely frightfully wrong.

"I must stop the making-short magic by giving her a make-people-tall magic," he muttered. "In fact, to make sure, I'd better giver her *more* than one make-people-tall magic, to make up for the making-short magic." But oh alas and everything, he hadn't brought any magic packets with him. They were all in the van which he'd turned into a scooter.

Frantically he dashed out of the room, slid down winding handrails, sprinted along corridors, out of the castle. But horrors, his magic scooter had vanished. Was there a rival wizard at work? No, no, the gardener had put it in the tool shed to make the place look tidy. At last William J found it. Turned it back into the van and dragon, hurriedly grabbed a handful of make-people-tall-magics, switched everything back to a scooter, shot back into the castle, sprinkled the magic powder on the Duchess and gabbled off the magic spell.

Only just in time. The next second the butler, three footmen and six mixed guards grabbed him and threw him out of the castle. But he managed to snatch up his scooter, turned it into an enormous bird and flew off.

Presently the Duke arrived, comfortably full of high-class lemonade and delicious chocolate biscuits.

"My goodness me, whatever is that?" he cried.

From inside the castle came a roaring noise like fifteen excitable lions roaring inside a tin tunnel.

"Can't be the hot-water boiler, that went wrong yesterday," he cried, "can't be the drains, we haven't got any, nor the fierce basilisk guard dogs, they're at the poodle parlour having their hair curled."

No no, it was none of these. It was the Duchess. She'd woken up to find herself twelve-feet high with a voice to match.

"Oh-oh-oh, what has happened," she wailed in a voice like two thunderstorms stuck together. "It's awful being as tall as this. I can see where the servants haven't dusted the ceiling. I'm conscious of cobwebs on the cornice. If I was my ordinary height I wouldn't have noticed these things so I needn't have worried about them. But now, oh-oh-*oh* everywhere looks positively filthy!"

The Duke ran round in circles of all sizes, wringing his hands, shaking his head and uttering so many cries of distress that the life-boat would have come out to him if it had heard him and if it could have got to him, which it hadn't and couldn't.

But why didn't he think of the magic he had in his pocket? Goodness gracious, though. He thought it was a make-people-thin magic and the Duchess was now quite thin enough for her height, in fact for a twelve-foot lady she was definitely on the skinny side. He wouldn't have thought it was any good using the magic he had with him. But oh-oh-oh, it was really a magic to make tall people short. It was just what was wanted. It would have made the Duchess the right size again, almost. But he didn't know.

"The wizard!" he cried. "I must find the wizard and buy another magic to put things right."

He dashed out of the castle even faster than the wizard had dashed into it. But where to find the wizard? Ha! He shot back into the castle and up to the watch tower, round and round and dizzily round the wildly winding stairs to the very upper top. He swept the countryside with a telescope.

Alas, the wizard had made himself invisible while he had his tea.

"Hm, what's sniff, this!" murmured the twelve-foot Duchess miserably picking up a packet from the floor.

What was it indeed? Good gracious, it was the packet of make-people-short magic. It had jolted out of the Duke's pocket while he was running round in circles.

"The way people leave things about," she grumbled. "Making the place untidy. I won't have it. I . . . ."

She opened the packet just as a gust of

wind came in through the window. Pouff! It blew the magic powder all over her.

"Oh, tut tut," she cried, then she caught sight of the magic spell printed on the paper that had held the powder. "What ever does this mean?" she growled. She read it out bit by bit to herself.

Of course, that did it. The make-people-short magic worked at once. *Zimmy-whizz-plop!* Instantly the twelve-foot-high Duchess became short. Oh dear, but not short enough. The wizard had used no end of packets of make-you-tall magic on the Duchess so just one packet of make-you-short magic wasn't enough to get her back to her right height. She was still nine-feet high.

"Oh, but I'm no fatter, that's something," she said looking down at herself. It was quite true. The make-you-short magic had made her shorter, and as she had been a bit skinny when twelve-feet high, she was now still a bit thinnish at nine-feet high.

But nine-feet high is still a bit too tall even for a Duchess. She had to stoop very low to go through doorways, and she wasn't the kind of Duchess who takes at all kindly to stooping low. She expected other people to do that.

Up on the watch tower the Duke suddenly caught sight of William J Waveywand and his magic van. He'd made himself visible again and started off on his magic selling journey.

"Guards!" yelled the Duke, rushing down the winding stairs and coming out at the bottom with his head still whizzing round. "Quick, follow me!"

The guards clambered onto their horses and shot off, led by the Duke.

"Faster faster!" cried the Duke. And "Faster faster!" shouted the guards, not having the faintest idea where they were going or what they were going there for, as the Duke had been in too much of a frantic hurry to tell them.

Down the main street thundered the Duke and the guards, round squares and through highways and bye-ways and avenues and groves. At last they came on the Wizard, his van and his dragon.

"Your magic's gone wrong," cried the Duke. "Duchess is nine-feet high."

"But not so fat?" asked William J Waveywand, hoping for the best but not expecting it.

"No no, not so fat," yelled the Duke, "but nine-feet high, it's nearly as bad! She has to have breakfast on top of the wardrobe and if she has to attend a banquet everybody else will have to go on stilts to keep up with her. Do something. Make Her Grace right size again."

"Um-er, um-umum," muttered the Wizard. Then he remembered something.

"I gave you a spell to make tall people short by mistake," he said. "All you have to do is sprinkle it on Her Grace."

The Duke clapped his hands to his pockets, which took a bit of doing as he had considerably many. But of course he couldn't find the make-you-short magic because he'd dropped it and the Duchess had already used it.

"I can't find it," he panted, "give me another."

But alas, the Wizard had sold out of make-you-short magics.

"I could let you have plenty of make-you-tall magics," he said, "then you you could make everyone else as tall as the Duchess which would be the same as making her the same height as everyone else."

"Pah!" snorted the Duke. "Do you think we want everyone nine-feet tall? Some of them are too big for their boots as it is. No no, think of something else."

The Wizard thought like mad. Smoke nearly came out of his ears. He scratched his head. He scratched the dragon's head, but that didn't help as dragons are absolutely no good at thinking of things.

"We shall have to use what magic we can," he said, "to work the Duchess round gradually to being right size again."

So back to the castle they all went and the Wizard started going through his various magics. He made her into two Duchesses, both nine-feet tall, one fat and one thin. He turned her into a grand piano with a very loud tone and then into a bookcase full of improving books. Then he changed her into a low coffee table and back into a Duchess.

"Good gracious," gasped the Duke.

For at last the Duchess was right size again, though a little on the short side, but she had a wooden leg, sort of left over from the coffee table.

"I'll soon put that right," said William J Waveywand, and after giving her a gold leg with diamond ornaments and changing that into a padded footstool, he managed to get the Duchess back to herself again, but thank goodness nice and slim.

"I don't know what I owe you in money for all that," said the Duke to the Wizard, "but I do know I owe you a powerful punishment for all the trouble you've caused us."

But William J Waveywand had vanished while the vanishing was good. And he and his magic van and his dragon were never seen in the Kingdom again, which was really just as well.

A Wizard by Mistake

Royal rejoicing and majestic merriment had broken out in the palace. For the King and Queen of Crashbania were going off to the seaside for a holiday. There was to be a grand banquet on the pier, brass bands on the promenade, red carpet at the railway station and free flags all round for people to wave.

"Give me that blue and yellow luggage label," said the Queen, "I bought it specially so that we shall know which is our royal trunk. It would be frightfully awful if we lost it and had no robes to attend the banquet."

"And no shoes to take off to go paddling without," said the King. "But it would be much worse if we had no banquet to go to." He felt most enormously hungry because the Queen had been in such a tear round, do-everything-at-once-where's-that-what-have-I-done-with-whatsname-find-me-the-so-and-so, there had been no time for tea, nor for dinner and only a munch and a gulp for breakfast.

The Queen had got them up so early in the morning that the King didn't know such a time existed. "We mustn't miss the train," she cried, bustling around doing everything three times over in case she forgot something.

"The train can't go without us," said the King, who was rather a one for a quiet life and taking his time and not being hurried, "the engine driver can't start until we give our gracious permission."

"Nonsense," gasped the Queen, writing a fifth note to the milkman saying not to leave any milk until next Tuesday week. "If he doesn't start the train on time we shan't get to Splashleigh-on-Sea in time for the banquet."

"OO-er," said the King, who hadn't thought of that. He clapped on his travelling crown, grabbed the Queen by the hand and shot off to the railway station in more of a hurry than the Queen herself had been.

"The train now waiting for the King and Queen," said a loudspeaker in very respectful tones, "is the non-stop, fast, special, luxury, get-there-quick royal train for Splashleigh-on-Sea."

"Tickets please," said a ticket inspector snapping his ticket clippers.

But of course the King and Queen didn't need tickets and the Station Master,

covered in gold lace like a highly fancy cake, shooshed him out of the way, bowed low to Their Majesties, opened the door of a super first-class carriage with carpet all over the floor and half-way up the walls. Closed the door and bowed again.

Trumpeters sounded a fanfare, nothing so un-royal as blowing a whistle, and the train started.

On the journey the King and Queen were served with an extremely majestic lunch but the Queen wouldn't eat any of it in case it spoilt her appetite for the banquet.

"I shall just nibble a bit," said the King, nibbling his way through a nice grilled sole, two chops, four potatoes, two helpings of cauliflower, five glasses of pink lemonade, two trifles and a chocolate cream bun.

At last they arrived at the seaside and drove to the Royal Hotel through streets lined with so many waving flags they couldn't see the people waving them.

"Well, here we are," said the Queen,

unfastening the trunk with the blue and yellow label.

"Where did you expect us to be?" asked the King. "I mean wherever we are it is bound to be here even if it was somewhere else. If we're there it must be here."

"Oh stop it," said the Queen. She flung up the lid of the trunk, let out a shriek like twenty-seven excited steam engines and collapsed into the King's arms. He collapsed into an armchair, which collapsed onto the floor.

There were no royal robes in the trunk. Absolutely none. Not even half a one, not that half a robe would have been much good between two people.

"But it can't be!" cried the Queen. "I packed them with my own hands." Goodness knows how she could have packed them with someone else's hands.

"Let me see," cried the King. He peered into the trunk and his eyes would have come out on stalks if they could have.

For inside the trunk were three strange-looking hats and a black stick.

"We must go back to the railway station," cried the Queen, "and see if they have our trunk there. Come on."

She dashed out of the hotel, followed by the King, who picked up the black stick to use as a walking-stick.

"The sea looks nice and calm," he said, "I wish we could go on it in a boat."

The next second there was a *whiz* and a *puff* and the King and Queen were sitting in a rowing boat on the sea.

"Well I never!" gasped the Queen. "Start rowing, Kingy, or we'll drift ashore."

The King took hold of the oars and splashed them about a bit, but he had no idea what to do with them.

"Oh I wish I could row," he cried, and immediately found he could.

"You never know what you can do till you try," said the Queen, then she added: "the sun's a bit hot, I wish I had a sunshade."

And *pop whizz* she had one, a very handsome sunshade in red and gold with fringe and tassels.

"What ever can be happening?" cried the King, rowing along like an expert. "Our wishes keep getting granted."

"I believe it's that black stick," said the Queen. "And those hats in the trunk. Perhaps they're magic."

Well of course they *were*. The trunk wasn't their trunk, it belonged to a Wizard. The hats were for taking rabbits out of. The black stick was his magic wand.

"Lovely!" cried the King. "Now we can have everything we want." He magicked himself an ice-cream-cone a foot long, stuffed with crystallised cherries.

"I wish for a nice iced lemonade," said the Queen, "and some cream cakes!" She was so hungry after no lunch she couldn't save up for the banquet after all.

Then, as those things arrived, the King wished the boat was a motor-boat, wished it would steer itself round and round and they both settled down to enjoy themselves.

In a cavern away on the slopes of the mountains of Mindasteppe, Wizzlepouf the Wizard was in several dithers.

"By all the borrowed watches in half the world," he growled, kicking at a trunk with a blue and yellow label, "there is some mischief afoot." He'd bought a blue and yellow label for his trunk to make sure of recognising it, and so that it shouldn't get mixed up with someone else's. But mixed up it jolly well had been.

How was he to know the Queen was going to have a blue and yellow label on the royal trunk? There are some things even a wizard can't be expected to know. Oh why couldn't he have chosen a red-and-mauve spotted label or a green one with black and white squares? Now he had the royal trunk, with no magic hats and worst of all, no magic stick.

"Somersaulting semolina!" he cried, as he felt a little "pop". "Someone has my magic stick and is making magic with it!"

Then another pop sounded. That was the King wishing he could row. It was followed by other pops as the King and Queen magicked themselves their own wishes.

"This must stop," yelled the Wizard. He didn't have his magic stick but he still had other magic powers. "I must undo that magic before it is too late," he cried.

Oh-oh, if only he'd known he was going to undo the magic while it was much too inconveniently early. But of course he didn't know. This wizard was jolly good at not knowing things. He made a pass. He chanted an incantation. He muttered spells.

Instantly the King and Queen were splashing about in the water. The boat vanished, so did the Queen's sunshade and the King's ice-cream-cone. Thank goodness they were in shallow water and could wade ashore, and the King managed to cling onto the magic stick.

"What's happened?" gasped the Queen

scraping seaweed out of her royal hair.

"Don't know," gurgled the King through a mouthful of sea-water. "But I wish we were back at the hotel and nice and dry."

"Pop" – back they were in a moment

"Now," said the Queen, "if only we had our robes on we could go to the banquet."

"I'll wish it," cried the King, waving the stick, "I'm sure this is some kind of magic stick."

He wished, and *swoosh!* Their robes were on in a jiffy.

"To the banquet!" cried the King, and off they went.

"Their Majesties the King and Queen of Crashbania," announced the Town Crier of Splashleigh-on-Sea.

Then in came the King and Queen, smiling and bowing to right and left and looking very special in their royal robes.

The next moment, *swish*, *zoom*, *bing!* Their robes vanished. The Wizard had heard the "pop" of his magic stick and undone the magic again.

Everything was awful. Thank goodness their majesties had some ordinary clothes on under their robes. But they were all crumpled through having been soaking wet and then dried again without being pressed.

Consternation took place. Panic happened.

The Town Crier dived under the banqueting table and bonked into the

Mayor who had dived under it from the other side. A Duchess fainted into a trifle. A frantic Earl hit a jelly and splashed ten Aldermen's sisters.

The King and Queen looked at each other and did what royalty must do on such occasions. They pretended nothing had happened. They sat down and the banquet began. But it wasn't really much of a banquet after that. You couldn't expect it to be.

It was midnight. The Wizard, in his mountain cave, was examining the trunk he'd got in mistake for his own and found the royal robes in it, where of course they'd returned when he undid the King's magic.

"Ramping rice puddings!" he cried. "This is awful. Their Majesties' robes! The trunk must belong to them. They will need their robes. I must magic them back."

He uttered spells again and *swoosh zim bing!* The King and Queen, fast asleep in bed, woke up to find they had their robes on.

"What ever did you wish that for, in the middle of the night?" gasped the Queen.

"I didn't," said the King. "But I'll soon put things right." He reached for the magic stick beside the bed and wished their robes off again and onto a chair.

But the Wizard heard the pop and instantly uttered another spell to undo the magic someone was doing with his stick. Of course he didn't know it was the King doing it.

So *zim bing* back onto the King and Queen in bed went the robes.

"Confound it!" roared the King and wished them off again. Next second they were back on them once more as the Wizard undid the magic.

Eighteen times they had to get up and magic their robes off again and eighteen times the Wizard wizzed them back.

"I've had enough of this magic business," growled the King at last. "Let's take the robes off unmagically."

So they did, and as there was no magic, the Wizard heard no pops and they were able to sleep in peace.

Next morning the Wizard arrived, bringing the royal trunk.

"Your Majesties," he said, bowing low and stroking his beard, "I fear by some mistake you have my trunk and I have yours. I trust you received your royal robes which I sent back by magic."

"Oh, you did, did you," growled the King, "so it was you that kept making us get up all night."

"Off with his head!" cried the Queen, helping herself to more marmalade.

"Oh, take your confounded trunk," said the King, "and your hats and your-er-your . . . Wait a minute," he said. He picked up the magic stick and went into another room and shut the door.

In a moment he returned and handed the stick to the Wizard, who bowed again, took his trunk, the hats and the stick and vanished in a puff of elaborately scented smoke.

"Well, thank goodness for that," gasped the Queen. Then she noticed a funny smile on the King's face.

"What were you up to in that room just now?" she demanded.

The King held out his hand and pointed to a strange-looking ring on his finger.

"Where did you get that?" asked the Queen.

"I magicked it up with the Wizard's stick," said the King. "It is a magic ring that will grant all our wishes. And . . ." he went on, "as it doesn't belong to the Wizard he can't undo the magic we do with it. Now let's magic ourselves up a nice royal yacht and go for a cruise!"

The Wizard who Lost his Temper

Herbert Howztrix was Court Magician to the King of Tarradiddledovia, and he was in several rages, two dudgeons, one high and one low and no end of a temper. Because the King wouldn't let him have a new cloak and wizard's hat.

"The mean old majesty," he cried, "the mingy monarch, the stingy sovereign. I've had this cloak and hat for so long they practically aren't there any more. There are more holes than cloak, and if the King had as little crown to his head as I have to my hat, he jolly well wouldn't be a king."

Of course Herbert Howztrix could quite easily have magicked himself a new hat and cloak, and very luxurious ones too. But that wouldn't have been right. In Tarradiddledovia the King himself had to present the Wizard with his hat and cloak.

For Herbert to magic it up himself would be like tapping yourself on the shoulder and calling yourself Sir something. Of course you wouldn't be a real knight at all if you did that. Most unjust and not at all satisfying. So Herbert had to wait for the King to be graciously pleased to present him with a new hat and cloak.

"Purple ones," he said to himself, "with green cats embroidered all over them. That's what I want and I mean to get them. Pah to the King!" and to show how furious he was, he turned an armchair into a raspberry meringue and stamped on it, squish.

Then he stalked off to find the King and arrived just as His Majesty was sitting down to a boiled egg with his tea.

"Can I have a new cloak and hat Majesty?" he asked for the twenty-somethingth time.

"No," said the King, getting ready to crack his egg.

"A thousand times no," added the Queen. She'd just ordered five new

dresses and thought it was time they saved somewhere, and that Herbert's hat and cloak were just the right place to do it.

"Pah!" snorted Herbert under his breath, which takes some doing, but he did it. Then he absolutely positively lost his temper and he made a magic. A frightful magic.

There was a puff of striped smoke and *whee-e-e-e bang!* The King's egg cracked with a noise like an explosion at a firework factory and out shot a spotted chicken the size of several elephants. Right through the walls of the royal palace it went, leaving the most noticeable hole.

"Now can I have a new cloak and hat?" screeched Herbert, a bit taken aback because his magic had gone much more sensationally off than he'd intended.

"To the dungeons with him!" roared the King.

Herbert didn't care, he put out a few spells and turned the dungeon into a very snug little room, with thick carpet, fancy curtains, soft armchairs, luxurious lights and a cupboard full of luscious food. He was just starting on a heavy tea, with kippers, cream cakes and fruit salad, when the guards burst in.

"Kindly knock before you come in," said Herbert, holding up his teacup very daintily with his little finger sticking very politely out.

"Ha," grunted the guards and hauled him away to the King.

"You must deal with this monstrous fowl you have created," cried the King, when Herbert stood before him on the terrace. "It is treading on houses and scratching up forests worse than any dragon."

"Can I have a new cloak and hat if I abolish the chicken?" asked Herbert, hopefully.

"You abolish this chicken or off with your head!" snarled the King.

The chicken trod on two villages and tore up a park and a half.

"Oh, all right," growled the King when he heard this news. "Abolish the chicken and you can have your new cloak and hat. Only mind you make a good job of it, and if you abolish yourself at the same time I shan't object."

"If I did that I couldn't have the new cloak and hat your Majesty has so graciously promised me," said Herbert, in a good temper again.

The King snorted and went inside the palace to be safely out of the way.

Herbert took a deep breath, drew himself up to his full height which didn't make him any taller though he thought it did. Then he slammed out a most tremendous magic spell to make the chicken so small that he could cook it for his dinner. *Tararárar bong whiz pouff!*

But, oh dear, he was so excited at the thought of having a new cloak and hat that he missed the chicken with the spell and hit the palace instead.

WHIZZZZZY ZIM zim *zim*. The palace shrunk down smaller and smaller until it was only three inches high. And the King shrunk down small with it, which was just

as well otherwise he'd have been mashed.

"Oh, oh, oh, *help!*" cried the Queen, rushing up from the rose garden.

Then the sky grew dark, as the chicken, still as tremendously enormous as before, came flying up.

"Fetch the artillery!" cried the Queen. "Fire, fire, fire!"

The tremendous chicken swooped down and picked up the little teeny palace with the little teeny King inside it, in his beak.

"Shoo, put it down!" shouted Herbert.

Then the fire brigade came clanging up thinking the Queen was calling for them when she shouted "Fire, fire, fire!"

The noise scared the chicken and it flew off with the palace. The King inside was shouting frantically out of a window

with his hair standing on end with fright, though he was so small it didn't notice.

Hurriedly Herbert magicked some wings on himself. They were odd ones and different sizes but he couldn't help that. He launched himself into the air and flew after the chicken, wobbling about among the sparrows.

The Queen rushed in all directions shouting for help. Ministers threw up their hands and didn't bother to catch them again.

Herbert was gaining on the chicken. Upside down, back to front, round and round he flew. Town and countryside see-sawed beneath him.

"We've reached the sea," he cried. With frenzied flaps he caught up with the chicken and grabbed its tail.

"Chic-a chic-chic *ooooo-wow!*" squawked the chicken. It turned to peck at Herbert and dropped the palace. Frantically Herbert magicked an enormous bunch of balloons on it so that it would float down gently.

Then he floundered down, managing to give the palace a push so that he and it came to rest on the edge of the cliff.

"Make me right size again this instant," squeaked the teeny little King from inside the palace.

"Yes, Majesty, of course, Majesty, at once Majesty," gasped Herbert. He made a hurried pass, muttered a swift spell and the King became full size again.

But oh-oh-oh how awful! He forgot to magic the palace full size again as well as the King. Bing crash, gazump *wallop*. As the King shot up to his full size he crashed through four ceilings. Doors and windows flew all over the place. "What is all this?" cried the King, scraping tiny furniture off himself and pulling midget carpets out of his ears.

The next second there was a terrific splash as the enormous chicken laid an egg as big as an airship in the sea. High tide occurred two hours too soon and a quarter of a mile too high, in defiance of all the best regulations.

The sea came rushing up the cliff and would have washed Herbert and the King away but they managed to cling to the notice that said: *This cliff is dangerous.*

"That's useful to know," grunted the King reading it over Herbert's shoulder, "we might have been at risk if we hadn't seen that."

"I'd rather be at home," wailed Herbert.

The chicken came whirring in for a low-level attack. Splosh, crump, *flop*, it laid a stick of huge eggs right across the cliff.

"Ya, missed . . . pooh!" shouted Herbert. The last exclamation was because one of the eggs was a bad one and smelt positively drastic.

"Magic that confounded thing away," roared the King.

But Herbert couldn't do it. He was clinging to the notice board with one hand and the King with the other. He couldn't make a magic pass without letting go, and he couldn't let go of the King neither could he let go of the signpost or they'd both have been washed away.

"Don't just cling there, *do* something!" spluttered the King, getting a mouthful of sea water.

Then the sun came out and turned the huge broken eggs into an enormous and highly smelly omelette.

The King managed to disentagle a hand from his robes and grabbed the signpost. Herbert let go of him and made a frantic pass in the direction of the chicken. It missed. He made another and yelped an incantation. The chicken split into five small ones that were still none too little and came flying back in formation.

Scree-e-e-e-e-ech plop plop plopetty *plop!*

Another stick of eggs, but thank goodness only as big as melons. Ow! More chickens came out of three of them. There was a whirl of wings. Assorted screeches broke out. Some of the chickens collided with others as they weren't much good at formation flying. Aerial fights broke out.

"For goodness sake magic us to safety," roared the King, who felt his fingers slipping from the signpost.

Herbert did his best. He incanted, he waved shaky hands, he let go spells.

Gradually he and the King rose in the air, drifted over dry land and dropped into a muddy pond. Just in time. A big wave sloshed over the signpost and washed it away.

But the chickens had re-formed and were whirring down on them. Eggs of all kinds showered down. Some were square, some were bouncy, some were explosive and all were smelly.

Then Herbert lost his temper again. "Perishing chickens," he cried, "frightful fowls, confounded cockerels!" He shot out a shower of spells to abolish the chickens but missed and hit a set of buses that were coming up the hill with the Queen and half the army.

"Pah," snorted Herbert, now in a regular rampaging roaring rage. He flung out another handful of spells and at last managed to turn the chickens into dust which the wind blew away.

"Now," said the King, when Herbert had calmed down a bit and magicked them both clean and dry from the muddy pond. "If you want your new cloak and hat you'd better get busy and magic up a new palace."

"No no no no!" cried the Queen, panting up, "for goodness sake don't let's have any more of this muddled magic business. Let's have a new palace built

slowly and properly in the ordinary way."

"What about my new cloak and hat?" asked Herbert.

"If you're not going to magic up a new palace you can't have a new cloak and hat," said the King.

"But I was going to magic up a new palace," protested Herbert, "only Her Majesty doesn't want me to."

"I not only do not want you to magic up a new palace," said the Queen, "I positively and absolutely forbid you ever to magic anything up again. This magic business is a forty-horse-power nuisance."

"But I want my new cloak and hat," wailed Herbert, "and how can I have them if His Majesty won't give them to me if I don't magic up a new palace and Your Majesty won't let me magic up anything?"

"That is a question I have no desire at all to answer," said the Queen sticking her nose up in the air but wishing she hadn't as she stuck it up too far and it hurt.

"Then I shall jolly well magic up a new cloak and hat my own self," cried Herbert, getting all ready to lose his temper again.

"It won't count if you do," warned the King. "A royal wizard's cloak and hat must be graciously presented by His Gracious Majesty himself, which is me."

"I don't care!" yelled Herbert beginning to wriggle his fingers.

"Stop!" cried the Queen. "I have an idea." She went across to the King and whispered in his ear.

"Um-ah, yes my dear, of course my dear," he said. Then he turned to Herbert.

"We shall be graciously pleased to grant you a new cloak and hat," he said in his best opening-of-parliament voice, "on condition that you promise never to do any real magic again, but only nice harmless conjuring."

"Oh, all right," said Herbert, who reckoned that was a bit tame but couldn't see any way out of it.

So Herbert went to live in a little house in the middle of a wood where he wouldn't disturb anyone. And all the magic he did was conjuring tricks with coloured handkerchiefs and knitted rabbits.

And the King and Queen, while their new palace was being built, went to stay with the Queen's uncle George. He had a nice semi-detached castle in the country with a rustic drawbridge and roses round the portcullis.

Wizards Strictly Prohibited

The Queen of Farrawania ran an enquiring finger along the mantelpiece to see if it was dusty. And it jolly well was.

She lifted a corner of the carpet to see if the dirt had been swept under it. And it absolutely had been.

She looked at the windows to see if they had been cleaned, at the furniture to see if it had been polished and neither they nor it had been.

"Disgraceful!" she cried. "This is no state for the state apartments to be in. There is nothing palatial about this palace. What my Auntie May would say about it if she were here I do not know, and as she isn't here there's no way of finding out, thank goodness."

"It's the servants my dear," said the King, coming out of a room with cobwebs on his crown.

"It can't be," said the Queen. "There aren't any."

"That's what I meant," said the King. "It's because the servants who aren't here are not doing any work that the palace is in such a mess."

"Well we can't get any servants, for love or money," said the Queen. "They like it better working in factories where they get tea breaks and holidays with pay and free pork pies or jars of jam or whatever it is the factory makes."

"I can't say I blame them," said the King, who was very fond of pork pies and simply enjoyed jam.

"Anyway, there's too much work in the palace," said the Queen. "Seven staircases, eighteen bathrooms, five larders, three-and-a-half coal cellars, drawing-rooms of all colours, state bedrooms by the dozen and enough passages to make a town full of streets. And the place is full of these silly ancient ornaments."

She picked up a strange-looking brass box covered in dust. But there was a spider sitting on it thinking about webs, so the Queen dropped it hurriedly.

Crash! The box hit the floor and burst open with a peculiar pop. Out of it came a cloud of mauve smoke followed by a long skinny gentleman in a pointed hat and waving whiskers.

"Behold, I am the marvellous Wizard of Wearizzit," he said in a very deep down voice. "Your Majesty has summoned me and I am here to do your bidding. What are your Majesty's most gracious commands?" He bowed low and produced a bunch of roses from nowhere, handed them to the Queen but they turned into butterflies and flew out of the window.

"Good gracious!" exclaimed the Queen. "What do you mean, I summoned you? I did nothing of the kind. And you're making the place look even more untidy than usual – which is hardly possible."

"Here," said the King, "this won't do you know. This 'Majesty has summoned me,' 'what are Majesty's commands' business is no business of Wizards. That's for Genies that is." He knew his fairy tales, did the King. It was the only thing he'd really learned at school.

"Your pardon, Majesty," said the Wizard, bowing low again, "but that is an old-fashioned idea if you will permit me to say so. Genies are out of favour nowadays. They are not with it, as the saying goes. Or rather I should say they are with too much of it. People don't care for them bursting up through the floor and scorching the carpet. People are frightened when an enormous Genie in a turban, with ear-rings the size of cartwheels, pops up in front of them. And besides, their ideas are so wholesale. You have only to ask one of them for something to eat and *wham* –" the Wizard waved his hands – "a frightful great banquet enough for fifty people appears. You can't eat it all and you have to live on warmed-up leftovers for a month. No no," he shook his head, "Genies are definitely out, your Majesty. How much nicer to have a quiet,

well-behaved Wizard to obey your commands."

"Oh well-er-er," said the Queen, "I see what you mean but . . ."

"Will Your Majesty be graciously pleased to say what Your Majesty graciously wishes to command of me," said the Wizard, "and for goodness sake hurry up," he finished suddenly, "I left an egg boiling and I dislike hard-boiled ones."

"Well," said the Queen thoughtfully, wondering whether perhaps she should seize the opportunity of getting no end of delicious dresses and heaps of harmonious hats magicked up while she had the chance. But she decided to be very noble and put the housework first.

"I should like," she said, "some way of getting the housework done nice and easily without anyone having to do it."

"With pleasure, Majesty," said the Wizard, "nothing easier, Majesty." He pointed with a long skinny finger to a sort of bell push affair on the wall by the grand staircase.

"I've never seen that there before," said the Queen.

"Tut tut," said the King, "you mustn't say 'that there', it isn't good grammar."

"I didn't say that there,' said the Queen, saying it again, "I said I'd never seen that button there before, or that's what I meant."

She looked round for the Wizard, but he'd disappeared.

"Well, let's try the new getting-housework-done-without-doing-it business," she said, and pressed the button.

Instantly the carpet rolled itself neatly up, invisible vacuum cleaners swallowed the dust out of sight and the carpet laid itself out again all nice and clean.

"Lovely!" cried the Queen clapping her hands. "Now let's have a look at the bedrooms." She went upstairs and sure enough there was another button she'd never seen before, on the bedroom wall. She pressed it.

The furniture promptly stacked itself up

in the middle of the room. The curtains took themselves down, cleaned themselves and went back of their own accord. Dust and dirt vanished. The furniture put itself back in its various places and the whole room was spick and span, shiny bright, spruced up and looking like new, all in a mere several seconds.

"Good gracious!" cried the Queen, not thinking she ought to believe it, but having to as she'd seen it all happen.

And it was like that all over the palace. Everywhere a convenient button to press and *zing bing tarara!* Everything instantly cleaned and tidied up.

"Um," said the King, who reckoned life was going to be a bit uncomfortable with everywhere so outrageously clean and tidy.

Next morning the Queen woke up with a frightful start. Pandemonium was reigning in the palace and it certainly knew how to reign. Uproar was occurring. There was enough noise for three and a half wars and ten protest meetings.

She started to run down the stairs. Oo-er! The King was rolled up in the stair carpet like an expensive and astonished sausage roll.

"Help!" shouted the Queen. She tore along to the throne room. The Lord Chamberlain and the Lord Chancellor were buried under the furniture.

She raced along the passage and found the Prime Minister fastened up behind a picture of himself. She scrambled into the hall where the Lord Chief Justice, two cabinet ministers and five royal guards were in the umbrella stand out of the way while invisible hands clankily polished the suits of armour.

Everything was goodness knows what. The palace was upside down wrong way round and inside out. It was like spring cleaning, moving day, and the French revolution all going on at once, twice over.

Her Majesty dashed round pressing every button she could see.

Things got worse, which was very nearly impossible but not quite. Armchairs piled themselves on top of one another, fell over with a catastrophic crash and began piling themselves up again. Two wild feather dusters who had no respect for age, began chasing a grandfather clock round the drawing-room.

"Help! Help!" cried the Queen dodging dining tables, getting out of the way of sideboards and only just missing beds as the frenzied cleaning went surging on.

A grand piano slid down the handrail and tried to get up the chimney. The Queen clambered up onto the mantelpiece and knocked the brass box down again.

"Pop!" cloud of mauve smoke. The skinny whiskered Wizard appeared again.

"Your Majesty wishes to wish another wish?" he asked, rather indistinctly as his mouth was full of hard-boiled egg, which wasn't polite but he hadn't been expecting a call.

"Yes, help!" gasped the Queen. "Stop all this at once. I wish I'd never wished anything."

"You need a little practice," said the Wizard, "these magic things take some getting used to. You pushed too many buttons too many times. Your second wish is granted, Majesty."

He waved a skinny hand. The furniture went back into place, the carpets stopped misbehaving. The King was let out of the stair carpet. The Prime Minister came down from the picture and the Lord Chief Justice, cabinet ministers and the guards escaped from the umbrella stand.

"Thank goodness for that," cried the Queen. "Thank goodness for some peace and quiet."

But she spoke too soon. At that moment there was a ring at the front-door bell and three Genie sort of people stood on the mat. One had a purple turban, tremendous ear-rings and too many teeth. Another had his head on upside down and the third had wings on his feet and scales on his chest.

"We've come from the United Genie's Association," said the first.

"It's a kind of thing like the Scouts and the County Council only a bit different," said the second.

"You have a Wizard working for you as a Genie," said the third, "and you must not ask him to do the things you are asking him."

"You are supposed only to command noble things," said the second Genie.

"Like laying waste your enemy's kingdom or slaying frightful dragons," said the first one.

"Housework is definitely out," put in the third Genie, "too degrading, not at all noble, most undignified and not genteel enough for a Genie."

"Nonsense," said the Wizard.

"What say?" asked all three Genies in surprise.

"You're talking nonsense," said the Wizard. I'm not a Genie and I don't belong to your stupid association. I am a Wizard of the first degree and only standing in for a Genie because you people are short of staff. I am not bound by your rules."

"You stop it or we abolish you," said the first Genie.

"You can abolish yourselves," retorted the Wizard.

"Now, now," said the King, who could see trouble coming, "do you mind doing your arguing outside. The Palace has just been cleaned."

"Conjure yourselves up a lake and jump into it," said the Wizard. "Unwind that turban, throw it into the air, climb up it and disappear, then pull it up after you."

The Genies were furious. Steam came out of their ears. They changed colour

several times. Oriental insults flew through the air like bad-tempered leaves in a tornado.

"We abolish you!" screamed the Genies.

"You and who else," snorted the Wizard. He turned the first Genie into a sausage, then turned the second one into a dog, who ate the sausage.

"Villain," yelled the third Genie, bringing the other Genies back again, a bit the worse for wear.

Then began the most uncalled-for dust up. Sparks and spells and sorceries flew in all directions. The Queen tried to hide under the grand piano but there wasn't room as she was definitely on the large side. The King called the guards but they'd seen what was going on and pretended not to hear.

Whizz bang crash zimmy plop!

At last the three Genies and the Wizard gradually vanished, still insulting one another, leaving behind a strong smell of cough mixture and burnt-out fireworks.

"Oh dear, I hope that's the last of them," panted the Queen. "But what a pity, after we were just getting all the housework done so nicely."

"Pooh," said the King, who didn't reckon being rolled up in the stair carpet was at all a nice way to have the housework done.

Then the Queen had a sizzling idea. "Listen," she said. "We may not have any servants, but we definitely do have a lot of royal guards. And there's nothing for them to do because there's nobody for them to guard us against, except the people who pay twenty-five pence to see over the state apartments on Thursdays and they aren't really dangerous. Well," went on the Queen, "as there's nothing else for them to do, why shouldn't the royal guards do the housework?"

"Coo!" gasped the King, "wouldn't that be rather dis-royal and un-majestic."

"Who said they had to be royal and majestic," said the Queen. "If they can polish their armour they can polish the furniture. If they're good at cleaning up an enemy they ought to be just as good at cleaning up the palace."

"I only hope we don't get a visit from the United Royal Guards Society telling us we mustn't do it," said the King.

But it was all right. The guards didn't at all mind doing the housework because it was warmer sweeping and cleaning inside the palace than stamping about outside, and a lot drier when it was raining.

But the Queen could never really get used to having her early-morning tea brought in by a whacking big soldier with a sweet little pink apron over his armour.

And if ever you should visit the kingdom of Farrawania, you'll find outside the palace gates an enormous notice that says in very large and determined letters: WIZARDS STRICTLY PROHIBITED

Other books in the same series:

Arabel's Raven
The Barrow Lane Gang
Brer Rabbit Stories
The Elm Street Lot
Dragons
Jack Stories
Icelandic Stories
Islands
The Lion and other Animal Stories
Littlenose
Littlenose Moves House
Littlenose the Hero
Littlenose the Hunter
The Quest for Olwen
Robin Hood
The Saturday Man
Stories from Ireland
Stories from Poland
Stories from Russia
Stories from Scotland
Stories from Wales
Voyage of the Griffin
The Wilkses

Jackanory Library Editions

The Adventures of Brer Rabbit: Twenty stories including the seven from *Brer Rabbit Stories*.

The Adventures of Littlenose: containing *Littlenose, Littlenose Moves House* and *Littlenose the Hero*.

The Pedlar of Swaffham: twelve traditional tales from the British Isles.

Also obtainable are the BBC Roundabout records of favourite Jackanory stories – Roundabout Nos. 5 and 7. Recommended retail price £1.00 from your local record shop.